SNAKES SET I

DIAMONDBACK RATTLESNAKES

Megan M. Gunderson
ABDO Publishing Company

visit us at
www.abdopublishing.com

Published by ABDO Publishing Company, 8000 West 78th Street, Edina, Minnesota 55439. Copyright © 2011 by Abdo Consulting Group, Inc. International copyrights reserved in all countries. No part of this book may be reproduced in any form without written permission from the publisher. The Checkerboard Library™ is a trademark and logo of ABDO Publishing Company.

Printed in the United States of America, North Mankato, Minnesota.
042010
092010

 PRINTED ON RECYCLED PAPER

Cover Photo: Getty Images
Interior Photos: Alamy pp. 5, 9, 18; Corbis p. 21; National Geographic Stock p. 11; Peter Arnold pp. 14–15, 17; Photo Researchers p. 19; Photolibrary p. 7

Editor: BreAnn Rumsch
Art Direction & Cover Design: Neil Klinepier

Library of Congress Cataloging-in-Publication Data

Gunderson, Megan M., 1981-
  Diamondback rattlesnakes / Megan M. Gunderson.
      p. cm. -- (Snakes)
  Includes index.
  ISBN 978-1-61613-435-8
  1. Eastern diamondback rattlesnake--Juvenile literature. 2. Western diamondback rattlesnake--Juvenile literature. I. Title.
  QL666.O69G864 2011
  597.96'38--dc22
                              2010013420

CONTENTS

DIAMONDBACK RATTLESNAKES . . . 4

SIZES 6

COLORS 8

WHERE THEY LIVE 10

WHERE THEY ARE FOUND 12

SENSES 14

DEFENSE 16

FOOD 18

BABIES 20

GLOSSARY 22

WEB SITES 23

INDEX 24

DIAMONDBACK RATTLESNAKES

Have you ever heard the rattle of a deadly rattlesnake? That warning sound tells you a **venomous** reptile is near! As reptiles, these poisonous snakes are vertebrates. Like all snakes, scales protect them from their enemies. And, stretchy skin lets them eat big meals!

Snakes are cold-blooded creatures. That means their surroundings affect their body temperature. Getting too hot or too cold is harmful. So, snakes lie in the sun to warm up. To cool down, they find shelter.

All rattlesnakes belong to the family **Viperidae**. The eastern diamondback rattlesnake and the western diamondback rattlesnake are two members of this family.

The rattlesnake gets
its name from the rattle
on the end of its tail.

SIZES

There are more than 30 types of rattlesnakes. Of these, the western diamondback rattlesnake is the second largest. The largest is the eastern diamondback rattlesnake!

Western diamondbacks average three to four feet (1 to 1.2 m) in length. The longest western diamondbacks reach seven feet (2.1 m).

Average eastern diamondbacks reach three to five feet (1 to 1.5 m) in length. They weigh around five pounds (2.3 kg). The biggest eastern diamondbacks grow much larger. These giants reach up to eight feet (2.4 m) long. They weigh up to ten pounds (4.5 kg)!

*Eastern (above) and western diamondbacks are
the longest and bulkiest rattlesnakes.*

COLORS

Just like their name suggests, diamondback rattlesnakes are covered in a diamond pattern. Dark diamond shapes with lighter borders run down the western diamondback's back. The eastern diamondback's markings are brown to black with white edges.

These patterns contrast with the snake's main body color. Western diamondbacks can be brown, gray, brick red, or straw yellow. Eastern diamondbacks are olive to blackish brown to dusty gray. Both species have light stripes on their heads. These extend back from their eyes.

These snakes also have striped tails. The western diamondback's tail has black and white or black and gray rings. It looks like a raccoon's tail.

So, the western diamondback is also called the coon-tail rattler. The eastern diamondback's ringed tail may be black and white or brown and white.

The western diamondback's diamond-shaped markings fade toward its tail.

WHERE THEY LIVE

Thanks to their special coloring, diamondback rattlesnakes blend into many **habitats**. Both eastern and western diamondbacks live mainly on the ground.

Eastern diamondbacks live in forests, **savannas**, and prairies. They also like abandoned farm fields. Western diamondbacks live in mountains, **plains**, deserts, forests, and **grasslands**. They are often found near rocks and boulders.

In these areas, eastern diamondbacks take shelter in old animal burrows. Western diamondbacks like burrows, too. They **hibernate** in them during cool winter weather.

Eastern diamondback rattlesnakes will live near wet areas such as swamps.

WHERE THEY ARE FOUND

You can find rattlesnake species all the way from Canada to Argentina. But, rattlesnakes are most common in the United States and Mexico. That's where eastern and western diamondbacks live.

Eastern diamondback rattlesnakes live in coastal areas of the southeastern United States. They are found from Louisiana to Georgia. They live throughout Florida. And, they are found as far north as North Carolina.

Western diamondback rattlesnakes live much farther west. They are found from California to Arkansas. Their range extends south into Mexico. They even live on islands in the Gulf of California.

Detail Area

Where Diamondback Rattlesnakes Live

NORTH AMERICA

Atlantic Ocean

Gulf of California

Gulf of Mexico

Pacific Ocean

N

SENSES

When you think of a snake, do you picture it flicking out its forked tongue? The snake does this because its tongue helps it smell! The tongue picks up scent particles in the air. Back inside the mouth, the tongue enters the Jacobson's **organ**. This organ determines what the odors are.

Snakes also have a sense of hearing. But, they don't listen through **external** ears. Instead, their lower jaws pick up vibrations in the ground. These vibrations travel up to the inner ears. In this way, snakes can tell if predators or prey are approaching!

As pit vipers, eastern and western diamondbacks have another special sense. Two heat-sensitive pits sit between the eyes and the nostrils. They help the snake detect **warm-blooded** prey, even in the dark!

A snake's eyes are especially sensitive to movement.

DEFENSE

Camouflage helps protect eastern and western diamondback rattlesnakes from their enemies. The special colors and patterns of their scales lets these snakes hide in their surroundings. Yet if they are discovered, diamondbacks will fight back!

When threatened, a diamondback rattlesnake rattles the end of its tail. That warning sound comes from loosely connected hollow **segments** of old scales. The snake also coils up and raises its head above its body. If that's still not enough, the snake strikes out. It bites with long, sharp fangs!

Young eastern and western diamondback rattlesnakes face many threats. They must watch out for large birds, carnivorous mammals, and even other snakes. Adults only face danger from human threats. These include automobiles, capture, and **habitat** destruction.

A western diamondback rattlesnake can raise its head up to 20 inches (50 cm) above its coils.

FOOD

Like all snakes, eastern and western diamondbacks are carnivorous. They devour mice, rats, squirrels, and birds. Western diamondbacks also eat lizards, insects, and toads.

Diamondback rattlesnakes sit and wait for prey to wander by. They also actively hunt down their meals.

These snakes kill prey with their long fangs. A western diamondback's fangs grow up to one-half inch (1.3 cm) long. An eastern diamondback's fangs can be twice that length! These hollow fangs **inject**

Diamondback rattlesnakes usually eat their prey headfirst.

venom into prey. This deadly poison kills small animals quickly. It is also dangerous to humans.

After biting its victim, the snake lets go. Then, it follows the prey using its tongue and heat pits. Once the prey dies, the snake swallows it whole!

If untreated, diamondback rattlesnake bites can cause death in humans.

BABIES

Like all rattlesnakes, eastern and western diamondbacks give birth to live young. The young are usually born in late summer. The size and number of baby snakes depends on their mother's size.

An eastern female gives birth to 6 to 21 babies. Each little snake measures 12 to 15 inches (30 to 38 cm) long. They weigh 1 to 2 ounces (35 to 49 g). A western female has 4 to 25 babies at a time. Each one is 8 to 13 inches (21 to 34 cm) long.

Diamondback babies are born with one rattle **segment** on their tails. Within a week, they **shed** for the first time. Each time they shed, a new rattle segment is added.

A snake usually sheds its skin in one big piece. This happens whenever the snake's skin becomes too small or worn.

The number of rattle **segments** won't tell you how old a rattlesnake is. This is because **shedding** may happen more than once a year, especially when snakes are young. And, rattle segments can break off over time. In **captivity**, diamondback rattlesnakes have lived 20 to 30 years.

GLOSSARY

captivity - the state of being captured and held against one's will.

external - of, relating to, or being on the outside.

grassland - land on which the main plants are grasses.

habitat - a place where a living thing is naturally found.

hibernate - to spend a period of time, such as the winter, in deep sleep.

inject - to forcefully introduce a substance into something.

organ - a part of an animal or a plant composed of several kinds of tissues. An organ performs a specific function. The heart, liver, gallbladder, and intestines are organs of an animal.

plain - a flat or rolling stretch of land without trees.

savanna - a grassy plain with few or no trees.

segment - any of the parts into which a thing is divided or naturally separates.

shed - to cast off hair, feathers, skin, or other coverings or parts by a natural process.

venom - a poison produced by some animals and insects. It usually enters a victim through a bite or a sting. Something that produces venom is venomous.

Viperidae (veye-PEHR-uh-dee) - the scientific name for the viper family. This family includes copperheads, rattlesnakes, and common adders.

warm-blooded - having a body temperature that is not much affected by surrounding air or water.

WEB SITES

To learn more about diamondback rattlesnakes, visit ABDO Publishing Company on the World Wide Web at **www.abdopublishing.com**. Web sites about diamondback rattlesnakes are featured on our Book Links page. These links are routinely monitored and updated to provide the most current information available.

INDEX

B

babies 20
body 8, 16

C

camouflage 10, 16
cold-blooded 4
color 8, 9, 10, 16

D

defense 4, 16

E

ears 14
eyes 8, 14

F

fangs 16, 18, 19
food 4, 14, 18, 19

H

habitat 4, 10, 16, 17
head 8, 16
heat-sensitive pits
    14, 19
hibernation 10

J

Jacobson's organ 14
jaws 14

L

life span 21

M

Mexico 12
mouth 14

N

nostrils 14

P

pit vipers 14

R

rattle 4, 16, 20, 21

S

scales 4, 16
senses 14
shedding 20, 21
size 6, 18, 20
skin 4

T

tail 8, 9, 16, 20
threats 4, 16, 17
tongue 14, 19

U

United States 12

V

venom 4, 18, 19
vertebrates 4
vibrations 14
Viperidae (family) 4